Do You Take This... Name?

The Bride's Complete Guide to Choosing and Changing Her Name

~

Christine Arnison

American Literary Press, Inc.
Five Star Special Edition
Baltimore, Maryland

Do You Take This... Name?
The Bride's Complete Guide to
Choosing and Changing Her Name
Second Edition

Copyright © 1997 Christine Arnison

Library of Congress
Cataloging in Publication Data
ISBN 1-56167-379-X

Library of Congress Card Catalog Number:
97-073453

Published by

American Literary Press, Inc.
Five Star Special Edition
8019 Belair Road, Suite 10
Baltimore, Maryland 21236

Manufactured in the United States of America

*T*ABLE OF *C*ONTENTS

Part 1: Will You or Won't You?

PART II: Changes and Notifications

$\mathscr{A}$CKNOWLEDGEMENTS

I owe many thanks to friends and family who were not only supportive of, but also enthusiastic about this book. Special thanks go to Steve Trattner for his invaluable counsel, Gail Nelson and Jose Bandujo who so generously shared their time and expertise, Terry Black for his wickedly thorough proofreading, Susan Malone for editing & encouragement, Merle Coyle for research, Jennifer Lapp, who endured endless re-writes, and some very special friends (you know who you are) whose unfailing honesty in their critiques saved me from wrong turns and unpardonable gaffs.

Most especially I am grateful to Enid Traub, my partner in writing the first edition, and the bride who had the inspiration.

$\mathcal{F}$OREWORD

I decided to change my name three years ago and began the slow process. What a nightmare! If only someone had given me THE BRIDE'S GUIDE, it would have saved me a great deal of time and aggravation. Nobody advised me of that "most useful tip: Be Consistent!". Well, I was anything but consistent! Sometimes I used my maiden name as my middle name, and sometimes I did not. I changed my address with some organizations but not with others. My most embarrassing moment was when a clothing store refused to accept my check because the name and address on the check did not match exactly with the name and address on my credit card and driver's license. In all, there were three different names and two different addresses! It was only then that I realized the importance of consistency.

THE BRIDE'S COMPLETE GUIDE TO CHOOSING AND CHANGING HER NAME provides a comprehensive and easy-to-read blueprint for changing your name. The phone numbers alone would have saved me countless hours of time. This book is a valuable resource and a <u>must</u> for any woman contemplating a name change.

Jill Milloy
Washington D.C. Attorney

Part One

Will You
or
Won't You?

Introduction

Congratulations! These will be exciting and sometimes hectic days as you prepare for your wedding. Some of that preparation includes considering the name you will use after marriage. What are the alternatives? What have other women chosen? What do they have to say about their choices?

Countless women have pondered these questions. Every year more than two-million marriages take place. And, while nearly 90% of the brides take their husband's names, the decision of whether to do so and the consideration of the alternatives are, to varying degrees, common to all.

Until now no single source for information or advice on this subject has existed. That is why I have researched the information available and surveyed women—and men—of different ages and professions from all over the country. Herein lies their advice and experiences, along with some perhaps surprising name-alternatives.

I hope you will find what follows informative and useful.

" 'This must be the wood,' she said thoughtfully to herself, 'where things have no names. I wonder what'll become of my name when I go in? I shouldn't like to lose it at all...' "

Lewis Carroll, THROUGH THE LOOKING GLASS

CHAPTER ONE

𝒯HE 𝒞HOICES

SHOULD YOU CHANGE YOUR NAME?

"...girls nowadays, are not brought up with a single eye to matrimony, as they used to be. At this end of the century one is first a woman, then a possible wife. There is one's own life to be lived, apart from the partnership that may be entered into by and by. The idea used to be that it was a wife's duty to sink her individuality completely, and live only for her husband..."
Mrs. Humphry, MANNERS FOR WOMEN

Those words were written by Mrs. Humphry at the end of the 19th century, not the 20th, but they might have been written today. Yet our freedoms extend even further than she—or any woman of her day—could have imagined, for today we can even choose our own names.

Only in the past two decades have marriage and divorce laws changed to allow a woman to consider and chose the surname by which she will be known. As women have increasingly gained recognition in their own right, so has the inclination to retain their own names increased. In 1992, *The Wall Street Journal* cited statistics that showed that fewer than three percent of all women do NOT take their husband's name upon marriage. In 1994, an *American Demographics Magazine* poll placed that non-traditional group at ten percent. Whether the numbers have changed or the statistics are more accurate is difficult to say. Neither do the numbers reflect the variations and inventive approaches brides and their husbands have found to settle the question of name. Nor do they provide insight into the considerations for making the choice, or the ramifications of that choice.

To find this information I interviewed hundreds of women, asking what choice they made and why, what they experienced as a result, and what they would say to other women making this important decision. They were extremely generous with their time and enthusiastic in their desire to provide insights. Their responses follow throughout these pages.

WHERE TO BEGIN

We might begin, as the Caterpillar of ALICE IN WONDERLAND did, by saying '*Who are you?*'. The choice you make and how you evaluate the alternatives will be influenced by such things as age, occupation, a previous marriage, whether you have children now or expect to, your religion, family traditions, your future goals, and many other factors of which only you can know.

If previously married, you may have additional influences affecting your choice, depending on whether you are widowed or divorced, and the views you have developed from your experiences. Most especially you will want to consider your children from a previous marriage, and the effects a change in your name may have on them and their lives, as well as on future children from your impending marriage. Remember that the grandparents of your children will also be affected. As you read on, watch for the ramifications and consequences that certain choices may have for them.

"What do you call yourself?" the Fawn said at last. "I wish I knew!" thought poor Alice. She answered rather sadly, "Nothing, just now." "Think again," it said, "that won't do."
Lewis Carroll,   THROUGH THE LOOKING-GLASS

Just what are the choices? They are no longer limited to maiden name, husband's surname, or a hyphen between the two as a creative variation. Following is a range of choices described by survey respondents and interviewees. All are reflective of the empowerment of women, the increasing involvement of husbands in creating a family unit, and the continuing changes in today's American society.

CHAPTER TWO

The Traditional Mr. and Mrs.

"Will you, won't you, will you, won't you, will you join the dance?"
Lewis Carroll, ALICE IN WONDERLAND

The overwhelming choice of brides remains the traditional one of taking their husband's name after marriage. At least 90% of all brides follow this practice. And according to some sources, tradition is reasserting itself and that number is increasing. The reasons are compelling.

In spite of society's spirit of willingness to allow the unconventional in the choice of names after marriage, its rules and conventions still favor the traditional choice. The first assumption on the part of most people will usually be that your married name and your husband's are the same, and that it is his. The forms completed, applications and reservations made, admissions and memberships granted, will all most likely be expecting information that reflects traditional names. Following tradition prevents confusion for insurance carriers and the schools your children attend. The IRS will be delighted with the conformity and your life will have one less complication. You will avoid countless situations requiring explanation of the difference in your name and your husband's, and which name goes with whom.

That this choice will provide expediency and easy acceptance in nearly every aspect of your lives together is not in question. And it is often for these very reasons that the great majority of women go this route. "The solidarity and ease of having a common [traditional] choice was the most comfortable decision for both my husband and me," wrote one woman. Another, who married after establishing herself as an accomplished business woman well known in her field, pointed out that she disliked her maiden name and "marriage was a wonderful excuse to retire it." She continued by saying she considered herself a feminist, but was "surprised at how easily I 'became' my new name." Now the mother of two children, she feels she has further reasons to be pleased with her decision, "I am very glad that I share my name with my children. It would be very hard for me emotionally if my whole family had one name and I had another."

Some women worry that changing their names will cause them to lose the identity they have established professionally. You will find more information about the choice of keeping your maiden name further on, but one observation merits inclusion here. A highly successful consultant took issue with the idea that a name change could damage her professional standing and cause a loss of clientele, even temporarily. She explained that she used the name change as an opportunity to talk to people and increase her name recognition. It gave her an opening—a conversation starter—and she found her recent marriage and new name made a strong impression on those with whom she spoke. She called it "the greatest sales tool I've ever found."

If you have no nagging doubts about giving up your name, if you do not risk some loss of recognition in your career or profession, and if you are comfortable in the tradition of taking your husband's name as a surname for you and your children, this is the right choice for you. If you have doubts, read on...

CHAPTER THREE

𝒯HE 𝒩ON-𝒯RADITIONAL CHOICES

A SIMPLE HYPHENATION

The Gnat...settled again and remarked "I suppose you don't want to lose your name?" "No indeed," Alice said, a little anxiously.
Lewis Carroll, THROUGH THE LOOKING-GLASS

Memorable as a marriage ceremony can be, the abruptness of moving from one name to another in a matter of moments can be a little difficult to adjust to. Maybe you just need some time. Or, perhaps your colleagues and clients would accept the change more easily if it were gradual. Many women accomplish this by simply using the maiden name with their new married one as if it were a middle name, then ultimately dropping it.

Other women use the hyphenated version—maiden name-husband's name—to form what the British refer to as a "double-barreled" name. If the result is a lofty and brief "Harriet Smythe-Beale", you are fortunate, but still in for some frustrations. If, on the other hand, the result approaches something awesome like "Millicent Hinckelforth-Dostoyevsky", you would do well to consider the ramifications and practicalities.

Even with a name like Smythe-Beale (or a still simpler, Smith-Brown), you will spend a great deal of time repeating, spelling and explaining your name, confirming the existence or absence of a hyphen, and getting it corrected when it inevitably turns up wrong in print. You will have problems with standardized forms (and there are so many of them) because they will not accommodate a hyphen-

ated name. As with most western societies, we are regulated, catego-
rized and filed by the use of forms, and these forms are limited in
space (most government forms allow 15 characters for the surname)
and, in the U.S., there is little or no provision for such things as
hyphens. If you choose to use a hyphen, you might notice it goes
missing at times, or that your name becomes truncated to only the
first part of your hyphenated name or, more interestingly at times,
with the addition of part of the second name.

In any case, your name will be incorrect. Some form-devotees
will simply tell you they cannot accept a hyphen or a name longer
than so many letters. Depending on the organization, you may have
little or no recourse for amending the abbreviated name that results.
In the case of a driver's license, some states will simply require you to
adapt your name to the limits of the form and the size of the license.
This may be true of other forms as well. Be aware that in some
instances, such as an insurance card, an incorrect name can put you
at risk of being refused treatment or coverage.

Be prepared to resort to only one of the hyphenated names
and, like it or not, your husband's will be the least troublesome. If
you are tempted to assert your right to have your name represented
as you wish—that is, correctly—by all means do so, but have patience and reasonable expectations; the flexibility of most standard
systems (computer and otherwise) has its limits for the exception.
Note that in the case of Ms. Hinckelforth-Dostoyevsky and others
of similarly long names, no known form in the western world will
accommodate a name of such length.

If you are a paragon of patience and a gifted teacher, this choice
will give you many exhilarating opportunities to demonstrate your
talents. If not, fortify yourself for a life of challenges. I received
interesting observations from women who decided on hyphenation.
One woman's experience is representative of most. She wished to
retain the name by which she had been professionally known for
over 20 years, and also wished to share her husband's name. She
observed that "hyphenating names *always* raised eyebrows, and often

snickers, and people tend to stumble over pronunciation—even if the name is as simple as Smith-Jones." She also wryly noted that the hyphenation allows for an "ease in transition if one changes one's mind—in either direction."

Before moving on, a few more points need consideration. A growing number of men are taking an active part in the choice of a surname to be used after marriage. One result is that some husbands also take the hyphenated name so it is the same as the wife's. With this option comes the choice of which name will come before the hyphen and which after. If this is a possibility for you and your husband-to-be, do give some thought as to whether you will be having children, and consider some possible outcomes. The first is that your children will undergo all the challenges and frustrations that you do, if they carry a hyphenated name. And secondly, complications may arise for your children when they are ready to marry. Consider, for example, the dilemma of Willie Henckelforth-Dostoyevsky and Camilla Smythe-Beale when they fall in love and decide to marry. Camilla, of course, wants to keep her own name—let us hope Willie does not!

⇠ ⇥◈⇤ ⇢

A NAME FOR ALL SEASONS

"Who are you?" said the Caterpillar. "I-I hardly know, Sir, just at present— at least I know who I was when I got up this morning, but I think I must have changed several times since then."
Lewis Carroll, ALICE IN WONDERLAND

I have known a few admirably well-organized women who have managed to use their maiden name for professional purposes and their husband's name in social situations—and still know who they are at the end of the day. Others who have tried this eventually ended up open-mouthed in confusion when pressed to introduce themselves. Social and professional situations are not always so clearly delineated. Which name to use? For those friends and situations that fall into the gray area, confusion over your dual-identity may occur for everyone, including yourself.

If you can juggle a dual-identity, this option could work for you. But you must keep one thing straight—your legal papers. Your name must be consistent across all legal and identity records, such as employer, social security, passport, driver's license, deeds, insurance policies and other important documents. (See the chapters on changing your name for details.)

Some women questioned whether this is actually a choice, or rather a way to avoid a decision. Certainly, using both names is another of the options that allow for a change of mind at a later point. Regardless of why you may consider this choice, if you plan to have children, give some thought as to what their surname will be.

⇢ ⊨✦⊨ ⇠

MY OWN NAME

"...'This must be the wood,' she said thoughtfully to herself, 'where things have no names. I wonder what'll become of MY name when I go in? I shouldn't like to lose it at all...'"

Lewis Carroll, THROUGH THE LOOKING GLASS

In the 18th century, Thomas Campbell wrote, "Who hath not owned, with rapture-smitten frame, the power of grace, the magic of a name?" In a time when women may assert their talents and gain recognition in their own right, many do not wish to relinquish their names. The artists and musicians with whom I spoke were most concerned with losing their names and public identities. They usually kept their names. Women in the professions, and executives in business also share this concern, but they were more likely to consider a name change or hyphenation.

Children, whether existing or planned, should be particularly considered in making this decision. Many survey respondents admitted they did not give this enough thought. "...Try to think of possible future considerations, not just current conditions...personal, social, professional, family, etc.," said the mother of two little girls. "Think about children," said another, "and how you will name them;

whether it's important to share their name…" One mother of two small boys had been married previously and was determined to keep her own name the second time. She knew she wanted children and considered seriously how her choice could affect them. She concluded, "I believe in choice and want my children to respect that…" Along with other mothers, however, she added numerous cautions.

All of these women had tales of hospitals and insurance companies that used their husband's name causing, in one case, the name of the woman to be unknown at hospital admissions. Frustrated friends and relatives who knew she had had a baby, found contacting her difficult. Similarly, insurance claims and coverage were denied these women, including the one just mentioned, because the hospital or insurance company assumed the husband held the policy (not always true, especially for working women) or simply used his last name in filling out forms.

Another concern involves children's safety. Although many children today have names that differ from one or both parents for various reasons (and society and its institutions are becoming more accustomed to this), it is important that the names of both parents be known by schools and child-care professionals. Unfortunately, to protect children from strangers is necessary today. Many schools will not allow a child to leave with a person claiming to be the father or mother, if the name differs from the child's and is unknown to the school. That the parent's place of employment know if children have a different name is also important, since an emergency call might need to be directed to a parent whose name differs from the child's.

Women without children have also experienced the same difficulties with forms, organizations, and institutions that have trouble accepting a married woman with a name different from her husband's. They, too, cautioned that women who make such a choice must be vigilant that their names are recorded correctly. Canceled insurance policies and IRS audits can be the result of errors or confusion.

Some will simply insist that the husband's name be used. As one woman expressed it, "I relent for convenience." As I learned while researching the chapters in Part 2 on name-change notifications, consistency is critical. In those chapters you will find many cautions for keeping records straight and information on possible consequences of inconsistency. To review them may prove helpful.

Most of the survey respondents who retained their maiden names were committed to their choice. I should note, however, that one or two, after having children, were thinking about taking their husband's name. Their reasons were based on family unity and a wish to reduce the confusion and frustration that being different sometimes causes. But the majority would agree with the words of an artist who had children from a first marriage (and had taken her husband's name) and then married a second time, keeping her own: "If you strongly identify with your maiden name and like it, as I do, keep it. The obstacles encountered are a small price to pay in order to maintain one's sense of identity."

CHAPTER 4

The Inventive Choices

The Duchess said "...and the moral of it is—'Be what you would seem to be'—or, if you'd like it put more simply—'Never imagine yourself not to be otherwise than what it might appear to others that what you were or might have been was not otherwise than what you had been would have appeared to them to be otherwise.'"

Lewis Carroll, ALICE IN WONDERLAND

Once, no choice about what name would prevail after marriage existed. With the Women's movement, equal rights, and so many women with careers of their own, things have changed. Marriages have become more balanced with men and women sharing responsibilities for earning, household chores and child-rearing. The idea of marriage as a partnership and a friendship is more commonly accepted today. Thus that men have become involved in the name issue, with some interesting results, should come as no surprise. But while the Duchess, I am sure, knew exactly what she meant, being emphatic in her confusion made her message no clearer to others. And a non-traditional name may similarly cause confusion for your friends and family. The alternatives described below will no doubt require more careful preparation and explanation than any other mentioned so far.

MY NAME IS YOUR NAME;
YOUR NAME IS MY NAME?

"Must a name mean something?" Alice asked doubtfully. "Of course it must,"
Humpty-Dumpty said.

Lewis Carroll, THROUGH THE LOOKING-GLASS

In some instances, the husband has taken his wife's maiden name and dropped his own. In the days when family fortunes were entrusted to sons who were responsible for "carrying on the family name", this could never have happened. But even in tradition-steeped Britain a woman's name could dominate if it were of a more prestigious lineage. Today the reason might be that a woman's name would be lost if she were the only descendent. Perhaps her husband has brothers to carry on his own family name and he is not committed to keeping it. Or a man may have no strong attachment to his name (or it is unappealing to him) and happily trades it for his wife's.

In *The New York Times Magazine* of May 14, 1995, the *Times'* Houston bureau chief Sam Howe Verhovek wrote of his choice to take his wife's last name when they married. Mr. Verhovek acknowledges it was not "a traditional move", but points out it was "for the most traditional of reasons. We wanted to hang on to the Verhovek name."

Whatever the reasons, a man may certainly be the one to make the change. It may be rare, but it has been done!

A TOTALLY NEW NAME

"They're putting down their names," the Gryphon whispered... "for fear they should forget them..."

Lewis Carroll, ALICE IN WONDERLAND

Finally we come to a new twist altogether. For the truly brave and seekers of the "path not taken" there is the choice of inventing a new name. Approaches include using a name from a past generation in either family, combining parts of each spouses' names—first, last, or middle—or taking (or making up) a name completely unrelated to either spouse. A couple, then, not only takes on a new life together, forming a new "unit", but actually a new identity.

One couple began marriage with a hyphenated name, his surname first, hyphenated with her maiden name—they liked the sound of the "reversed" order best. This name selection, however, was not their final decision—they wanted to live with it for a while and consider whether they would have children, and if that might influence their name choice. At the time I spoke with them they were, in fact, considering a <u>new</u> name—one different from either of their surnames.

There is something romantic, as well as pioneering, about this approach. It is symbolic of the new entity the couples will form when they marry, and expresses the commitment they both make to that new, unified entity. On the more practical side, it by passes some of the difficulties encountered with hyphenated names or spouses having different names, although it does pose a temporary identity challenge for both partners who will spend at least their first year together re-introducing themselves to friends and family. And although the children will share the parent's name, they will not share the names of any grandparents and here lies one of the cautions. Resistance may surface from parents and grandparents—even resentment. To anticipate this would be wise. Prepare your families for this step, should you choose to take it. Also worth considering is what the genealogical implications of inventing a name could be, should some future generation attempt to discover its past.

Such are the non-traditional choices. Each one has a varying degree of challenge and frustration attached. Being different usually does. It is to this aspect that I now turn.

"...They don't seem to have any rules in particular: at least, if there are, nobody attends to them—and you've no idea how confusing it is..."
Lewis Carroll, ALICE IN WONDERLAND

CHAPTER 5

THE ETIQUETTE OF BEING DIFFERENT

"...that's not a regular rule; you invented it just now",
Lewis Carroll, ALICE IN WONDERLAND

Just what are the rules for using non-traditional names? There are few, if any. By slipping the bonds of tradition we have lost its guidance. The result, of course, is confusion.

The road seldom traveled has its hazards, providing obstacles and frustrations along the way; some anticipated, some not. In all cases, patience will serve you well. Our society allows for choice, but does not guarantee that no consequences will ensue for "bucking the system."

"Take the responsibility of informing people of (your) decision," suggested one woman who had chosen to take her husband's name, but had watched several of her friends fume and fuss when people "thoughtlessly" assumed they had taken their husbands' names when, in fact, they had retained their own. Such "social assumptions" are frequent and will cause a great deal of frustration unless, as this woman counseled, you can be "...understanding and comfortable with politely correcting people who will just assume you've taken your husband's name." Her words represented the conclusions of all of the women I heard from who have made an unconventional choice.

One very wise suggestion was to carefully consider the feelings and reactions of both families. Parents and grandparents may have difficulty understanding even a "conservative" non-traditional choice. Take the time to talk with them about your thoughts and gradually introduce them to your decision. Your consideration will spare them confusion and, perhaps, hurt feelings—yours and theirs.

The etiquette books do provide some authoritative guidance, though no established standards are in place. Letitia Baldridge and Emily Post suggest that non-traditional names be noted in an "at home" card enclosed in a wedding announcement (not the invitation, admonishes Miss Post). Miss Post also suggests the last line of the wedding announcement in your newspaper as an appropriate place to state explicitly what name the bride, or couple, will have after the wedding. Wedding correspondence and stationary should also bear the correct name. And Miss Baldridge suggests that in social situations introductions be made clearly and carefully so that people have time to hear a name that may be different from what they are expecting.

Judith Martin, in the person of Miss Manners, has responded to several questions from confused brides, their families and friends. She advises tolerance if one is incorrectly addressed, and patience while providing the correct name.

In a newspaper column from a few years ago, Miss Manners provided some very helpful counsel:

> *Miss Manners has a deskful of letters from people who cannot get themselves properly addressed by the names or honorifics they prefer.*
>
> *She has neatly sorted them by the likely causes:*
>
> *Confusion (such as not understanding hyphenated names, or how to address couples in which the lady uses a professional title socially);*
>
> *Disapproval (deliberate misuse of someone else's choice, often accompanied by such tiresome cracks as the Mrs. "means her husband owns her");*
>
> *Malice (inequality in usage that seems to be connected with race or gender);*
>
> *Misguided Friendliness (unauthorized liberties such as using first names, making up nicknames, or inappropriate endearments);*
>
> *Ignorance (unfamiliarity with the customs of a particular profession, or even with standard usage);*
>
> *Forms of address are being adapted and invented at a great rate, and it is difficult to keep up with the variety of available choices. Miss Manners advises the misaddressed first to presume mistakes are honest.*

A surprising number of people who are angry when their preferences are not respected actually are keeping them a secret.

You must give others a fighting chance by telling them what your choice is at every opportunity—birth announcements, wedding correspondence, notes mentioning changes at the time of divorce, formal names on writing paper, introductions and signatures.

Those who have names that are difficult to pronounce or to spell, who have changed their names or abandoned their nicknames, will have to resign themselves to going through life providing the correct information.

And finally, misuses will have to be politely set straight.

This excellent guidance will serve well for anyone considering a choice outside of our societal expectations.

AND THE NAME IS...

The experiences of the women I spoke with clearly confirm that there is no "best" or "right" choice. The decision on the name you will bear is both a private and an individual one and one to be made jointly with your future husband. It is also a decision with broad family and social implications. I hope these pages have helped you to make it an informed decision, and one you will make with confidence

What's in a name? That which we call a rose
By any other name would smell as sweet.
William Shakespeare

Part Two

Changes

and

Notifications

The only sense that is common in the long run, is the sense of change—and we all instinctively avoid it.

E.B. White

CHAPTER 6

*I*NTRODUCTION

If you have made the decision to change your name, a bit of work lies ahead for you. Perhaps you haven't given much thought to how to go about making the changes, i.e., what exactly needs to be done and where to get the information.

The following pages provide that for you. I've spoken with hundreds of people in all the places that need to be notified when a name is changed. You will find the who, what, when, where, and how of changing your name. You will also have the benefit of many insights, hints and advice, as well as cautions, from the experts.

A CHECKLIST AND CHANGE RECORD (Appendix B) is included in this book, which will help you keep track of all the notifications you may need to make. A quick scan of this list will provide an idea of the range of organizations you will want to notify, and will ensure that you don't forget anyone! Once completed, it will serve as a handy reference for all your account numbers, policy numbers, and other personal data, for future use. Also included are samples of a simple notification card (Appendix C) to make things a little easier.

While this "housekeeping" exercise is not as much fun or as exciting as the many other activities you have to look forward to, it is a very important part of the preparations for your new life. This book just makes this task easier.

The following chapters have been organized to provide quick reference, as well as comprehensive information:

HELPFUL TIPS provides the best of the suggestions and advice gained from my research. Some of the tips are repeated in other parts of the book where they have specific impact.

NAME CHANGE NOTIFICATIONS covers all you need to know about notifications for changing your name. Information is included on how and where to make the notifications, and what you will need to satisfy each organization's requirements.

QUICK REFERENCE BOXES summarize key information for each category and special items of interest are found in the TAKE NOTE! boxes throughout the book. Notification categories include:

KEY NOTIFICATIONS: The ones that are most important to your legal identity, such as social security, driver's license, passport, immigrations, and your employer.

FINANCIAL INSTITUTION NOTIFICATIONS: Essential information for banks, credit unions, mortgage companies, investment companies and stock brokers.

CREDIT CARD NOTIFICATIONS: Retail, bank and gasoline company card-issuers that should be notified without delay.

INSURANCE POLICIES AND PROFESSIONAL NOTIFICATIONS: Insurance companies and professional services providers, such as doctors, lawyers, accountants, etc., who should be included in your more immediate notifications.

MEMBERSHIP NOTIFICATIONS: Auto clubs, frequent-flyer clubs, car-rental clubs, book clubs, health clubs, professional and alumni associations, video stores, video and music clubs, and investment clubs.

NOT TO BE FORGOTTEN: Notifications of less immediacy you will not want to forget, including voter registration, subscriptions, religious organizations, business associates, catalogues, magazine subscriptions, etc.

KEY CONTACTS are listed in each category. These identify the names, telephone numbers and, if appropriate, addresses of many of the organizations you will want to notify. Of necessity, these are organizations large enough to have central service centers. Some of your contacts, however, may be local or regional, which means you may have to find additional contact numbers. Where possible, suggestions are included for these contacts, as well. The KEY CONTACTS are also listed alphabetically in Appendix A to serve as a handy reference later.

◆─◆ ═◆═ ◆─◆

HELPFUL TIPS

Many of the experts interviewed provided valuable suggestions and tips. Some of these tips were to make a process easier, and some were cautions of problems that could arise if changes were not properly made. Many of them will be repeated later where they are most pertinent.

Of all the tips, the most valuable and frequently repeated was to be consistent. Once you've decided to change your name, notify everyone with whom you deal. There are many inter-relationships between the companies, institutions, and agencies we deal with every day. Wherever they cross information paths, an inconsistency with a name or identification number can cause unexpected hassles, from the irritating bureaucratic-type to the cancellation of an insurance policy, or the refusal of credit — even to being refused re-entry into the United States after a holiday abroad. Information in the following pages will help to ensure that the hassles will be minimal and the "disasters" never occur.

MOST USEFUL TIP: BE CONSISTENT! CHANGE YOUR NAME IN THE SAME WAY AND WITH ALL ORGANIZATIONS.

MOST ORIGINAL TIP: MARRY A MAN WITH THE SAME LAST NAME.

Following are important things to keep in mind:

Request at least 4 certified copies of your marriage certificate. The offices that issue copies vary from state to state. Some are issued by municipal offices, some by county offices. The person who performs your ceremony will know. The cost also varies but seems to range mostly from $7.00 to $15.00 per copy.

Make several photocopies of your marriage certificate. (If you do not have a copy machine available to you, you may find one at your post office, library, office supply store or copy center. Most charge between 5¢ and 25¢.)

Carry a certified copy of your marriage certificate with you during the first year or so of your marriage. It can save you time and hassle in those unexpected circumstances when you are asked for proof of identification or marriage.

Read instructions on forms, particularly government forms, such as social security, passport, immigration, etc. *very* carefully. Many are multipurpose forms, so first locate the name-change instruction section. Several identification documents may be required for submission with your form. An incomplete or incorrect submission is likely to cause delay in registering the name change and in having your documents returned.

✺ Be aware of accounts, policies, legal forms, etc., held by your husband which will need to have your name added. Don't forget to add his name to yours, too.

✺ Your credit rating could be affected by name conflicts and unpaid bills made undeliverable due to name and/or address changes. You can avoid that unwelcome surprise by reviewing a copy of your credit file from the credit bureau. Do this at least once a year to ensure its accuracy. (See A WORD ABOUT YOUR CREDIT RATING in Chapter 9 for more information about credit bureaus.)

✺ Misdelivered and undelivered mail can also cause insurance policies to be canceled if premiums are not paid on time.

✺ If any urgency arises to changing your record, as on a credit card, passport, etc., you may be able to use an overnight-mail service to expedite the documents. For those which do not require original documents or signatures, ask if they would be willing to accept information by fax.

✺ Remember to change beneficiaries on financial accounts and insurance policies.

✺ Use the CHECKLIST AND CHANGE RECORD to enter information about the changes you have made; you may have occasion to refer to the list if a change request is not made, response is slower than you expected, or if you have sent original documents that are to be returned.

✺ Order new name and address labels early and use them to change your name and address; they will make your work easier.

✺ If possible, make address changes at the same time you change your name. Check with your post office for change of address cards — they are free! If you remain at the same address but change your name, notify post office staff to ensure they do not think mail is being misaddressed. To avoid confusion, put a note on your mail box showing both your previous and married names.

❈ It can take as long as 8 weeks to process an address change on a subscription. While the post office will usually forward magazines at your request, you may want to begin those changes early. Enclosing an old address label with your new name and address speeds processing.

❈ Send notifications that require signatures and/or confidential information such as Personal Identification Numbers (PIN) and account numbers in an envelope so it cannot be read by anyone but the recipient.

❈ If you are interviewing for jobs, use this opportunity to contact employers with whom you have met and notify them of your change of name. It may give you that important extra visibility that can make the difference.

CHAPTER 7

Key Notifications

This category includes your Social Security registration, driver's license, and passport. Each of these is an important identification credential. Check thoroughly for accuracy. Also in this category are instructions regarding your employer and immigration documents.

SOCIAL SECURITY REGISTRATION

> ### *Quick Reference*
> - Obtain "Application for a Social Security Card" by calling 1-800-SSA-1213
> - Submit completed form with certified copy of marriage certificate
> - May be done by mail or in person at local Social Security office
> - Complete before filing current year's income-tax return
> - No fee for change

Social Security numbers are used by the Federal Government to keep accurate records regarding your Federal Income Taxes, Social Security Taxes, and payments made to you under various Federal programs, such as retirement, Medicaid, Medicare, etc. Your government files are kept under the name used to register you for your social security number. When you change your name, as you may when you marry, you must notify Social Security of the change.

WHAT YOU WILL NEED
- The Social Security Administration's "Application for a Social Security Card" (Form SS-5) must be completed.
- Your original marriage certificate (or certified copy) is required.

HOW TO MAKE THE CHANGE

The "Application for a Social Security Card" can be obtained by calling 1-800-SSA-1213 (1-800-772-1213). Social Security will mail the form to you. The form includes clear instructions for its completion, and indicates what you will need to include. Your form will come with an envelope showing the appropriate address for its return with your papers.

You may also obtain, complete, and file an application by visiting your local Social Security office. Be sure to take your original marriage certificate (or certified copy) with you. To find the local office, call the toll-free number above or look under the Federal Government listings in the telephone directory. The number may be listed in a frequently-called numbers section at the beginning. If not, look for "Social Security", or under the heading "Health and Human Services" for your local office listing.

Your employer may be able to provide you with the "Application for a Social Security Card" form.

WHEN TO MAKE THE CHANGE

File immediately after your marriage and before filing your income taxes.

WHY MAKE THE CHANGE

Periodically, the Internal Revenue Service (IRS) reviews social security numbers. If a number and name are found not to match, the IRS will seek to reconcile the discrepancy. You may get a letter of inquiry, and your income-tax processing or refund check may be delayed. Some employers will not change their records until you are able to show them your new Social Security card with your name changed.

❦ TAKE NOTE! ❦

If you were born outside the United States, you must include proof of U.S. citizenship, or appropriate Alien Registration documents. **These documents must be originals.**

⋅—⋅⋇⟐⟤⋅⟐—⋅

DRIVER'S LICENSE &
AUTOMOBILE REGISTRATION

Quick Reference

- Change in person at local Division of Motor Vehicles
- Take current driver's license and certified copy of marriage certificate
- May need additional identification — call local DMV for requirements
- Change usually required within 30 days of marriage
- Automobile registration should be changed at the same time
- May be a fee for change

Your driver's license is an important and frequently used identification. You will want your license to reflect your correct name and address to avoid delays and hassles when proof of identification is needed. Regulations for driver's licenses are defined by each state, and practices vary as you will see in the information which follows.

WHAT YOU WILL NEED

In addition to your current driver's license, you will need a certified copy of your marriage certificate. Some states also require other proof of identification, such as a passport, original birth certificate or social security card. Telephone first to be sure you know what will be required.

HOW TO MAKE THE CHANGE

Changes to your license must be made in person at your local division (or department) of motor vehicles office. (Look in the state government listings in your telephone directory under Department or Division of Motor Vehicles (DMV) to find the most convenient location for you.)

WHEN TO MAKE THE CHANGE

Most states recommend that changes in name and address be made on a drivers license within 30 days. If you are stopped you may be asked to produce valid proof of your identity and residence. In some states a fine for driving without an updated license may be levied.

WHY MAKE THE CHANGE

Apart from division of motor vehicle requirements, conflicts in identification credentials may cause delays and questions in situations in which your driver's license is used for identity verification. For instance, if you have new checks, but have not changed your license, you may be delayed in cashing your check or it may not be accepted at all.

MOTOR VEHICLE REGISTRATION

Variations from state to state occur regarding how and when to change your motor vehicle registration. When you go in to change your license, the Division of Motor Vehicles can inform you whether you should take steps to change your registration information. It may be done automatically at the same time you change your license.

⟶ ⫸◆⫷ ⟵

UNITED STATES PASSPORT

> ### *Quick Reference*
> - Obtain "Passport Amendment/Validation Application"
> - Send completed form, current passport, and certified copy of marriage certificate to regional Passport office
> - Complete before traveling overseas (follow special honeymoon instructions in TAKE NOTE! below)
> - No fee for amendment of passport

If you travel abroad, your passport *must* be completely accurate. While you may go on your honeymoon abroad without changing your passport first, you may encounter serious difficulties at a later date. (See below.) All this is to say that your passport is a very important credential and should not be neglected when you change your records.

WHAT YOU WILL NEED

You will need a "Passport Amendment/ Validation Application" (Form DSP-19), which may be obtained at your local passport office, usually in the county courthouse or post office. (Check the Federal Government listings in your telephone directory under "Passport" in the frequently-called numbers section, or under the heading "U.S. Department of State" to find your nearest office.) You may ask that a form be mailed to you.

A certified copy of your marriage certificate is also required.

HOW TO MAKE THE CHANGE

You may change your passport in person or by mail.

Mail the completed form, the certified copy of your marriage certificate, and your passport to the regional Passport office nearest you. (A list of these offices appears on the back of the "Passport Amendment/Validation Application" form, along with detailed instructions for making the change.)

If the regional office is near you and you're in a hurry, you may wish to deliver the required documents and completed form in person. Call to find out the length of time to complete the process—it may be several days.

If you mail your documents, they and the amended passport will be returned usually within 25 working days. You may speed the return by including required postage fees for expedited delivery, usually $30. Also include a copy of your ticket and itinerary. Allow 10 days for expedite processing, or 2-3 weeks, if visas are required.

WHY MAKE THE CHANGE

For any foreign travel after your honeymoon you will need an amended passport. If questions about or conflicts with your identification arise, you can be refused entry to your destination, or re-entry into the United States.

❦ TAKE NOTE! ❦

- If you leave immediately on your honeymoon and your travel requires your passport, take a copy of your marriage certificate (obtained from the person who performed your marriage ceremony) along with your passport. When you return, follow the procedures for passport amendment, but obtain a certified copy of your marriage certificate to submit with the application.
- The Passport office advises you to take your passport and copy of marriage certificate even if you are going to Canada, Mexico, or the islands (except Hawaii).
- There is no fee for amending your passport.

⊷⊶ ⋈⧓⧓ ⊷⊶

IMMIGRATION

Quick Reference
- Call local Immigration and Naturalization Service (INS) for appropriate form depending on your status
- Have two identical photographs taken within 30 days of the application that meet the requirements set forth in the INS instructions
- Take completed form along with a copy of your marriage certificate and the two required photos, to the INS office (unless they instruct you to do otherwise)

If you were born outside of the United States and hold papers permitting you to reside in the United States, you must notify the Office of Immigration and Naturalization of any changes in name and address. You will need to complete specific forms appropriate to your residence status.

To find the appropriate contact, look in the U.S. Government pages of your telephone directory. If a frequently-called number section is included, look under Immigration and Naturalization Service (INS). In the complete listings you may find Immigration under the Department of Justice heading.

There are different forms to be used, depending on your residency status:
- If you have been issued a Declaration of Intention, Naturalization Certificate, Certificate of Citizenship, or Repatriation Certificate, ask for the "Application for Replacement Naturalization/Citizenship Document" (Form N565).
- If you are a permanent resident or conditional resident, ask for the "Application to Replace Alien Registration Card" (Form I-90).

WHAT YOU WILL NEED

Both forms require that you submit two identical color photographs, taken within 30 days of your application, which meet INS requirements.

Both forms require a copy of your marriage certificate. Unless an original is specifically requested at the time of filing, a photocopy is acceptable.

Both forms require the original "Service" document or alien registration card.

All of the above are to be submitted along with the completed appropriate form.

In the case of alien registration you will be asked to complete the signature and fingerprint blocks of Form I-89, Data Collection Form, at the INS Office where you file.

HOW TO MAKE THE CHANGE

You must appear in person at the INS office having jurisdiction over your place of residence. Note that you may be asked to mail in your forms and accompanying documents, after which the INS will contact you for an appointment.

WHEN AND WHY TO MAKE THE CHANGE

As with all documents that verify your identity, your immigration papers should be current, so changes should be made as soon as possible. Carry a certified copy of your marriage certificate with you to show with your documents until you have officially changed them.

FEES

The Application for Replacement Naturalization/Citizenship Document requires a fee of $50.00. Your check or money order should be made payable to the Immigration and Naturalization Service.

The Application to Replace Alien Registration Card requires a fee of $70.00. Your check or money order should be made payable to the Immigration and Naturalization Service.

(There are exceptions to these fees if you live in Guam or the Virgin Islands.)

❦ TAKE NOTE! ❦

- Read the instructions for the form carefully; they are very specific as to how to fill in the forms and what procedures to follow. Photographs are required in both cases and the specifications for them are given in detail.
- INS cautions that if an application is not signed or accompanied by the correct fee, it will be rejected. You may correct the error and re-submit the form.

━◆━

YOUR EMPLOYER

Quick Reference
- Notify key personnel and benefits administrators
- File a new W-4
- Change beneficiary designations as appropriate
- May need copy of marriage certificate (usually photocopy) and new Social Security card
- **Notify as soon as possible**

Your employer needs to have current and accurate information about you for the company records and to provide information to the government for your taxes and social security, to insurance companies for your benefits, to banks and financial institutions for paychecks or electronic funds transfers, and perhaps to investment funds for 401Ks, Individual Retirement Accounts (IRAs), etc. Obviously, to notify your employer of a name change as early as possible is important.

Each employer will have its own procedures for updating records, but you may have to take responsibility for informing more than one person or group of your change. Following are some suggestions.

WHOM YOU MAY NEED TO NOTIFY
- Personnel Office or Human Resources
- Benefits Office
- Payroll Office
- Savings Plan Administrator

- Mail Room
- Office Reception
- Key Secretaries
- Colleagues

NEW FORMS TO FILE
W-4s. Your employer will need these forms for tax purposes. By filing new forms you will effectively be notifying the Internal Revenue Service (IRS) of your name (and address) changes. You

may also want to change your deductions and filing status at this time. (Note that if your W-4 and Social Security card are in different names, the inconsistency will at some point trigger a request for clarification from the IRS and may delay income-tax processing.)

Health Insurance Forms. In addition to noting a name change, you may wish to add your spouse to your health insurance plan, which will require another form.

Beneficiary Designations. You may wish to make your spouse your beneficiary on life and accident insurance policies, pension and savings plans, etc. While in some instances a spouse automatically becomes the beneficiary of a policy or financial plan, you may wish to ensure that this is the case and complete new beneficiary forms.

REQUIRED PAPERS

Social Security Card showing your new name. Some employers may require this to see that the government has been informed of your change, and that social security and tax payments made under your Social Security number and name will match with those on file at the IRS.

Original, certified copy, or photocopy of your marriage certificate as required. (More than one may be required). This may be requested for changing benefits and beneficiaries.

Your employer may not require anything more than that a form be completed indicating your new name and address, and that you complete a new W-4. In any case, your personnel office will be able to explain the procedures and requirements for your company.

KEY CONTACT

If necessary, you can contact the Internal Revenue Service directly for W-4s and other forms. Call 1-800-829-1040.

❦ TAKE NOTE! ❦

- Don't forget to add your name to your husband's health insurance and make appropriate beneficiary changes.

- If you are self-employed make changes, as appropriate, to licenses, permits, insurance, 401K, associations and other documents and organizations particular to your profession. Follow the general guidelines of this section and remember that consistency is critical.

CHAPTER 8

Financial Institution Notifications

The information in this section includes procedures for banks, credit unions, lending institutions, investment companies and stockbrokers. If there's one thing you want to keep straight, it's your financial accounts and investments! The requirements for name changes vary considerably among these institutions, but important considerations apply to them all.

BANKS, CREDIT UNIONS & OTHER FINANCIAL ACCOUNTS

> *Quick Reference*
> - Call the institutions for requirements — they vary widely
> - Complete signature cards and provide copy of marriage certificate for all transaction accounts
> - Order new checks early
> - Change all accounts consistently

WHAT YOU WILL NEED

Signature Cards. Most of these institutions require a signature on file that reflects the way you sign your name. You will be asked to fill out new signature cards to update your file. If you want to add your spouse to your accounts, you can file both signatures at the same time.

Most likely you will need copies (sometimes certified) of your marriage certificate. In addition you may be asked to show other identification such as a driver's license, to authenticate the signature. **Check Order Forms.** For your checking (sometimes called "draft") accounts, you will want new checks printed showing your new name and, if applicable, address. Use the check re-order form furnished with your checks to request checks with the new information and (if appropriate) your husband's name. You will be charged the usual fee for new checks. By the time you begin using them, you should have a new signature card on file also. You need not supply evidence or proof of name change to order checks.

HOW TO MAKE THE CHANGE

Call your financial institution(s) before you need to make changes. They will give you their requirements, help you with the process, and speed things along.

Many banks require that the change be made in person. If this is the case, remember to take along the requested identification and proof of change (marriage certificate). If you are adding your husband to an account (or your name to his account), remember that both of you must complete signature cards.

Some institutions will allow you to mail your signature cards. Most also require a copy of your marriage certificate (whether certified copy or photocopy varies), and some will also ask for a photocopy of your driver's license.

WHY AND WHEN TO MAKE THE CHANGE

Refer to FOR ALL FINANCIAL INSTITUTIONS section which follows.

❧ TAKE NOTE! ❧

- You may want to order new checks before you are married because they take time to process. But be sure your signature is changed and on file before you begin to use them.

━━━━ ❈❈❈ ━━━━

LENDING INSTITUTIONS, BROKERS & OTHERS

WHAT YOU WILL NEED

For institutions that may not require a signature on file, such as a mortgage company, a written request accompanied by a photocopy of your marriage license may be sufficient.

Some financial institutions, such as those handling mutual funds, stocks, and bonds, have their own forms to be filled out, and they may have stricter requirements.

It is not uncommon for an "Affidavit of Name Change" form to be provided by the institution for your completion. It requires your new signature(s) to be notarized, especially if you hold stock certificates and bonds.

HOW TO MAKE THE CHANGE

Requirements vary widely so it is important to check with each institution for its procedures and requirements.

━━━━ ❈❈❈ ━━━━

FOR ALL FINANCIAL INSTITUTIONS

WHY AND WHEN TO MAKE THE CHANGE

Good reasons exist for making these changes as soon as possible:

• Differing names could impede applying for credit.
• You may be refused service if you are asked for identification and it differs from your account or check. You will certainly be asked to verify your true name and to wait for confirmation or authorization.

- A check sent in payment may be returned if the name differs from what is on record. The result could be a past due notice and a finance charge.
- Money cannot be electronically transferred to an account with a different name (for instance, from a stock or mutual fund account to your checking account).

❦ TAKE NOTE! ❦

- If you receive checks under your former name but have updated your accounts, endorse them with both names.
- Be sure to change all of your accounts. Don't forget savings, checking, Individual Retirement Accounts (IRAs), lines of credit, loans, etc.
- If you have an IRA, your spouse may automatically become the beneficiary, but you may want to fill out and submit a beneficiary-designation form. You must fill out a beneficiary-designation form if the beneficiary is to be someone other than your spouse.
- Remember that all interest earned and dividends paid are reported under your Social Security number to the Internal Revenue Service, so if you've changed your name in one place, it is best to change it in all.

UNITED STATES SAVINGS BONDS

U.S. Savings Bonds are exceptions to most of the above. If you choose, you may change your name on bonds you own by completing Form PD F 4000 ("Request by Owner of Reissue of United States Savings Bonds/Notes to Add Beneficiary or Co-owner, Eliminate Beneficiary or Decedent, Show Change of Name, and/or Correct Error in Registration"). This form may be obtained from your local bank or by calling 1-202-377-7700 or writing the Department of Treasury, U.S. Savings Bonds Division, Washington, D.C. 20226. If you want to add your husband as a co-owner or beneficiary, you can do this on the same form.

If you do not change your name but wish to cash in some bonds, you will only need to take them to a bank, along with a certified copy of your marriage certificate. (If the bank you use is also the bank where you have your accounts and you have made the necessary changes already, you may not even need the copy of your certificate.)

If you intend to hold your bonds for a long period and have not changed your name, at the time when you cash them you will be asked to endorse them with the name under which they were issued (your maiden or former married name) and current married name. Since bonds are tracked by social security number, which you will have updated with your married name, there should be no difficulty in cashing them.

CHAPTER 9

CREDIT CARD
NOTIFICATIONS

Thousands of credit cards are issued by countless businesses and institutions. This accounts for the many variations to the requirements for change-notifications. These variations are more easily explained by breaking the providers into three major categories:

- Retail Credit Cards (those issued by stores and catalogues)
- Bank Credit Cards (such as Visa and MasterCard)
- Gasoline Credit Cards

A call to the issuers of your cards may be necessary for you to determine precisely what is required. A list of addresses and (where possible) contact numbers for major card issuers may be found in the KEY CONTACTS section.

RETAIL CREDIT CARDS

Quick Reference

- Call the telephone number, usually toll-free, on your recent bill for requirements or call or visit the Customer Service office of your local store
- Have a copy of your marriage certificate available (a photocopy should work)
- Make changes as soon as possible to ensure bills will reach you and to protect credit rating

---

Retail credit cards are issued by thousands of merchants, from department stores to hardware, clothing and jewelry retailers. Catalogues also offer credit cards. Even if you don't use them frequently, your credit card information should be kept updated.

WHAT YOU WILL NEED

Of those companies that require proof of marriage, nearly all will accept a photocopy of your marriage certificate. You will need to mail or fax it to them.

Other requirements sometimes include your signature and social security number and, of course, your account number.

A few stores will ask you to fill out a form, which is usually available at the store, or can be mailed at your request.

HOW TO MAKE THE CHANGE

Most issuers will accept changes by telephone or by letter. Look on a recent bill for the telephone number and address to contact. (Check the KEY CONTACTS section for some issuers' telephone and address information.)

Some stores will process your changes at the Customer Service office. However, often this service involves little more than handing you the telephone after they have dialed the central Customer Service number. If they have no toll-free number, this could save you the cost of the call.

A few stores do have a very easy method: fill out the change of address section of your monthly bill and send it in as usual. Unfortunately, this is not the common practice, so be sure to check with your card issuers.

In most cases, you will receive a new credit card within 7 to 10 days.

WHY MAKE THE CHANGE?

Failure to change your name (and address) with credit card issuers may result in damage to your credit rating due to confusion of account information and misdirected bills that do not reach you for payment. Request a copy of your credit file from a credit bureau at least once a year to ensure its accuracy. (See A WORD ABOUT YOUR CREDIT RATING at the end of this chapter for more information about credit bureaus.)

🍎 TAKE NOTE! 🍎

- Many credit card issuers provide contact numbers, usually toll-free, on their monthly bills. Often these are regional numbers and differ from one part of the country to another, so be sure to check your bill and, if you move, note that the number may be different.

KEY CONTACTS

Beall's
1-941-747-2355

Bloomingdale's
1-212-705-2000

The Bon Marche
1-206-506-6000

The Bon-Ton
1-717-757-7660

Burdines
1-305-835-5151

Carson Pirie Scott
1-414-347-4141

Dillard's
1-501-376-5200

Elder-Beerman
1-513-296-2700

Filene's
1-617-357-2978

Foley's
1-713-651-7038

Gottschalks
1-209-434-8000

Hecht's
1-703-558-1200

Herberger's
1-612-251-5351

I. Magnin
1-800-726-3444

Jacobson's
1-517-764-6400

J.C. Penney
1-800-542-0800

John Wanamaker
1-800-333-0170

Kohl's
1-414-783-5800

Lazarus
1-404-913-4000
The Limited
P.O. Box 182123
Columbus, OH 43283
1-800-888-3257
Lord & Taylor
424 5th Avenue
New York, NY 10018
Attn.: Customer Svc
1-212-827-5200
Macy's
1-800-743-6229
Marshall Field's
1-312-781-1000
McRae's
1-601-968-4400
Mervyn's
1-510-785-8800
Montgomery Ward
1-800-289-9740
Neiman Marcus
1-214-741-6911

Nordstrom
1-206-628-2111
Parisian
1-205-940-4000
Peebles
1-804-447-5200
Rich's
1-800-241-0488
Robinsons-May
1-818-508-5226
Saks Fifth Avenue
1-800-221-8340
Sears, Roebuck and Co.
Call the toll-free number on
your statement
Spiegel
1-800-345-4500
Stern's
1-201-845-5500
Younkers
1-515-244-1112
Woodward & Lothrop
1-202-879-8000

BANK CREDIT CARDS

Bank credit cards are issued by thousands of financial institutions from the largest national bank to the smallest local credit union. Regardless of whose name is on the front of your card, it is backed by a bank, credit union,or other financial institution that extends the credit.

Generally, the larger issuers have the easiest requirements and the smaller ones often request more documentation to ensure identity. While this may add to your paperwork these requirements help the issuers protect you and themselves from theft and fraud. As with retail cards, requirements and procedures for changes vary widely.

WHAT YOU WILL NEED

Your account number, PIN (personal identification number), mother's maiden name or some other means of verifying your identity.

For those requiring written proof, a photocopy of the marriage certificate usually will suffice; original documents were rarely mentioned in our research.

HOW TO MAKE THE CHANGE

Call the customer service numbers for your cards (usually found on your bills) to ask about the specific requirements of your card issuers. Addresses and telephone numbers for some bank card issuers can be found in the KEY CONTACTS section below.

Your new card will likely be issued within 7-15 days.

WHY MAKE THE CHANGE

Failure to change your name (and address) on bank credit cards can affect your credit rating for the same reasons noted in the previous section for retail credit cards.

If your cards are registered with a security-assurance program, be sure to inform them of the changes, as well. In some cases the credit card issuer will be able to do that for you.

❦ TAKE NOTE! ❦

- Many requirements for name changes are governed by the issuers' concerns for fraud and theft. Most requirements help to protect both you and the issuer.

KEY CONTACTS

American Express
1-800-528-4800
AT&T Universal
1-800-423-4343
BankAmerica
Look for number on your
statement, if unsure, call
1-800-227-5458 or
1-800-243-7762

Chase Manhattan
1-800-441-7681
Citibank
1-800-950-5114
Diner's Club
1-800-525-9135
Discover Card
1-800-347-2683

GASOLINE CREDIT CARDS

Nearly all gasoline credit cards may be changed by calling the customer service number listed on your monthly bill or in the KEY CONTACTS section below. Many of these numbers are automated and you will need to have your account number handy.

In addition, some credit cards can be changed simply by filling out the change of address section on a current bill and indicating specifically the change of name as well as address, if appropriate.

If your card issuer also provides auto-club service and you are a member, call the club's toll-free number. In some instances you will be able to make changes to both your club membership and gasoline card at the same time.

KEY CONTACTS

Amoco
1-800-247-0067
BP
1-800-222-1005
Chevron
1-510-602-7020

Exxon
1-800-344-4355
Marathon
1-800-537-9580
Mobil
1-800-225-9547

Shell   Texaco
 1-800-331-3703   1-800-552-7827
Sunoco
 1-800-331-8850

A WORD ABOUT YOUR CREDIT RATING...
        Changes or inconsistencies in your account information can
lead to problems with your credit record. Request a copy of your
credit file from a credit bureau at least once a year to ensure its accuracy. Listed below are the three major credit bureaus and their policies. (All offer free copies if you have been denied credit in the past
60 days and the creditor used their service.)

Equifax Credit Bureau
1-800-685-1111
Equifax will provide copies of your credit file for a fee ranging from
$0 to $8.00, depending on your state of residence.

TRW Credit Bureau
1-800-682-7654
TRW will provide one free copy per year of your personal-credit file.
Additional copies may be ordered for $7.00 each.

TransUnion Credit Bureau
1-800-851-2674
TransUnion will provide copies of your credit file for approximately
$15.00 each, depending on your state of residence.

CHAPTER 10

$\mathcal{I}$NSURANCE $\mathcal{C}$OVERAGE
& $\mathcal{P}$ROFESSIONAL
$\mathcal{N}$OTIFICATIONS

Overlooking some of the organizations and people in this category is easy because they are generally not part of our day-to-day routine. Several months can pass without encountering any ramifications of failing to notify them. However, serious consequences can arise. Since many of these companies and professionals have fairly simple requirements, the time it takes to notify them will be well spent.

INSURANCE POLICIES

> ### Quick Reference
> - Telephone the insurer for specific requirements
> - If necessary, provide request for change in writing and include photocopy (if acceptable) of marriage certificate.
> - Include policy numbers on all correspondence and have them ready when speaking by telephone or in person

Among the notifications you will want to make without delay are to issuers of your various insurance policies, including:

- Life
- Accident
- Automobile
- Health
- Mortgage
- Homeowners/Renters
- Business

Some of these were noted in the EMPLOYER section of this book. When you contact the holders of your policies, be sure to ask about any beneficiary designations that might need changing, as well as any information needed if you are adding your spouse to the policies.

WHAT YOU WILL NEED

Some companies will take the change information over the telephone.

Some may ask that you send a letter notifying them of your name change, along with a photocopy of your marriage certificate. Be sure to include policy numbers. A simple message such as the one shown on the notification-card example *(Appendix C)*.

HOW TO MAKE THE CHANGE

Telephone the customer service department of your insurance company(ies) to learn their requirements.

WHY MAKE THE CHANGE

Policies can be canceled if bills for premiums are not paid. If you do not notify of name and address changes, bills may be delayed or returned. Questions of coverage or reimbursement for medical bills may arise if name discrepancies occur. Also be sure your deductibles are credited correctly after the change.

·— ≡✦≡ —·

PROFESSIONAL SERVICE PROVIDERS

Quick Reference
- Telephone the service provider for requirements
- Provide your telephone number, if new
- Update your name and address in person if you have an upcoming appointment
- Indicate you are also changing relevant insurance policies

You will want to notify the professionals who provide service to you of any name and address changes. Remember to consider:

- Doctors
- HMO/PPO
- Dentist

- Lawyer
- Accountant
- Financial Planner

If you do not expect an office visit within 6 months after your marriage, you may want to call them with your new information. Be aware that discrepancies between your name of record on your insurance policies and the name under which your doctors provide service and file claim forms can cause difficulty in processing a claim.

HOW TO MAKE THE CHANGE

Telephone your service providers or visit their offices to provide updated information.

Inquire if a specific form must be completed or identification/proof of marriage is required.

WHY MAKE THE CHANGE

Providers often submit information on your behalf to insurers, for government records and to other service providers. If your personal information is not consistent you may lose reimbursements from insurers, lose information relative to deductibles met, have difficulty getting service, or even have a policy canceled.

❦ TAKE NOTE! ❦

- This is also a good time to update your will, or have one drawn up if you have not already done so.

CHAPTER 11

Membership Notifications

Memberships come in many varieties and types. By consulting the CHECKLIST (*Appendix B*), you may refresh your memory of those you hold. Included are book clubs, health clubs, professional associations and alumni associations, libraries, video stores, video clubs and music clubs, investment clubs, etc.

With few exceptions, your memberships will not be jeopardized if you do not change your name on them immediately. For your own benefit, however, you may wish to notify them of any address change to prevent misdelivery of packages and information. The simplest of notifications, such as the sample card in *Appendix C*, will do. And you might as well tend to everything while you're in the process!

On the other hand there are a few memberships which require your attention more than others due to the potential impact of not providing current name and address information. Those include auto clubs, and car-rental and frequent-flyer memberships.

AUTOMOBILE CLUBS

Quick Reference

- Telephone local office or customer service number to make change
- Provide account number (for both accounts if combining memberships)
- Change beneficiary designations if insurance coverage is involved

---

WHAT YOU WILL NEED

Generally, your membership number will be all that is required.

HOW TO MAKE THE CHANGE

A telephone call will usually do it. Your membership card may have the number to call, or check the KEY CONTACTS section below.

If you choose to make changes by mail, be sure to include your account number and any information about your spouse and his membership, if you are combining memberships or adding him to yours. Ask if any additional fees or forms are required for additional membership cards.

Some auto-club coverage applies to only the club member, some to the automobile. This can make a difference as to how you are covered if you travel (for instance on your honeymoon).

WHY MAKE THE CHANGE

To maintain consistency in your identification, always notify your auto club. Check to see if your club requires that your driver's license, auto registration and membership all be under the same name in order to receive service. (Some do not.)

If you have insurance associated with your membership, notification is critical.

❦ TAKE NOTE! ❦

- If you are combining two accounts with the same club, you may have an advantage by keeping the membership of longest standing.
- Remember to change beneficiary designations if you have associated insurance with your memberships.

KEY CONTACTS

Allstate Motor Club
   1-800-255-2582 or
   1-800-347-8880
American Automobile Association
   (AAA). Call the number on
   your membership card or
   check the telephone directory using the correct local
   name such as "Automobile
   Club of Michigan" or "New
   Jersey Automobile Club". If
   unsure, call 1-800-222-4357
   and you will be referred to
   the correct local club.
Amoco Motor Club
   1-800-334-3300

Chevron Travel Club
   1-800-255-2273
Cross Country Motor Club
   1-800-225-1575
Exxon Travel Club
   1-800-833-9966
Mobil Automobile Club
   1-800-621-5581
Montgomery Ward Auto
   Club
   1-800-621-5151
Road America Motor Club
   1-800-262-7262
Shell Motorist Club
   1-800-621-8663

CAR-RENTAL CLUBS

> *Quick Reference*
> - Call customer service number for specific requirements
> - Signature and photocopy of marriage certificate may be required
> - Change as soon as possible to avoid delays at car rental counter due to confusion over identification

WHAT YOU WILL NEED

Many car-rental clubs require proof of change in order to alter your records. Often a photocopy of your marriage certificate is sufficient.

Some companies require that a signature accompany the documentation.

HOW TO MAKE THE CHANGE

Telephone the customer service center for your club(s) — some are listed in the KEY CONTACTS section below — to learn requirements.

A few companies will allow you to make changes at the counter when you rent a car; however, this is not the common practice.

WHY MAKE THE CHANGE

If the name on your membership does not match that on your driver's license, you can be refused a rental or delayed. Until your new card is issued, you can prevent this by carrying a copy of your marriage certificate.

New cards are generally issued within 10 days.

❦ TAKE NOTE! ❦

- As with retail and bank cards, many of the requirements for name changes on car rental and airline frequent-flyer programs are used to prevent fraud and theft.

KEY CONTACTS

Alamo Rent A Car
Quick Silver Club
1-800-732-3232
Fax: 1-800-851-5246

Avis Rent A Car System
Wizard Club
Customer Service Center
900 Old Country Road
Garden City, NY 11530
1-800-352-7900

The Hertz Corporation
#1 Club
P.O. Box 25991
Oklahoma City, OK 73126
1-800-227-4653

National Car Rental
Emerald Club
7700 Franc Avenue S.
Minneapolis, MN 55435
1-800-962-7070

⤙ ⚌◆⚌ ⤚

FREQUENT-FLYER PROGRAMS

Quick Reference
- Call customer service number for specific requirements
- Signature and photocopy of marriage certificate may be required
- Change as soon as possible to avoid loss of mileage credit

WHAT YOU WILL NEED

Nearly all clubs require that you submit evidence of your name change and your signature. A photocopy of your marriage certificate is usually acceptable.

HOW TO MAKE THE CHANGE

Telephone the customer service center for your frequent-flyer program to learn requirements. (In some cases the number is on the back of your card, but you will find many of them listed in the KEY CONTACTS section.)

WHY MAKE THE CHANGE

If you get airline tickets issued in your married name and the name on your account is still your maiden name, *you will not get mileage credits.*

❦ TAKE NOTE! ❦

- If you also belong to any airline clubs (private lounges found in many large airports), informing them of your name change will minimize confusion, especially if you make use of their ticketing assistance.

KEY CONTACTS

American Airlines AAdvantage
MD 5400
P.O. Box 619620
Dallas/Fort Worth Airport,
Texas 75261-9620
1-800-882-8880

Continental OnePass Service
Center
P.O. Box 4365
Houston, TX 77210-4365
1-713-952-1630

Delta Airlines, Inc.
Frequent Flyer Service Center
Hartsfield Atlanta Int'l Airport
Dept. 745
P.O. Box 20532
Atlanta, GA 30320-2532
1-800-323-2323

Northwest Airlines, Inc.
World Perks Service Center
P.O. Box 11001
St. Paul, MN 55111-0001
1-800-327-2881

TWA - FFB
P.O. Box 800
Fairview Village, PA 19409
1-800-325-4815

United Airlines
Mileage Plus Service Center
P.O. Box 28870
Tucson, AZ 85726-8870

USAir
Frequent Traveler Program
Service Center
P.O. Box 65
Winston-Salem, NC
27102-0065
1-800-USAIRFT
(1-800-872-4738)

＊＋ ≍◈≍ ＋＊

OTHER MEMBERSHIPS

The remainder of this category, such as memberships in book and music clubs, health clubs, alumni and professional associations, video stores, libraries, and investment clubs, may be notified by telephone or by a simple written notification (see the notification card sample in *Appendix C)*.

In the instance of libraries, health and investment clubs, video stores and others where you either have regular meetings or personal contact when you use your membership, you may make a change in person, generally without documentation.

CHAPTER 13

Not To Be Forgotten

Some name and address changes, while important, do not impact your day-to-day life or your identification. This final chapter includes this type.

Urgent action may not be required, but not changing them may result in annoyance. When you go to vote months from now and see your maiden name on the card, you'll realize you have one more thing to change — just when you thought it was over! You may also begin to miss your favorite magazine or catalogue. Even after you've notified them you'll still have a few weeks' wait while they change their records, so don't put down your pen yet!

VOTER REGISTRATION

When you change your name or move, you will want to change your Voter Registration. To vote under your new name you may need to be registered a specific time period prior to an election. Usually, if you are unable to do so, you may use your maiden name as long as you sign the register using that name.

In January, 1995, the new National Voter Registration Act (popularly known as the "Motor Voter Law") went into effect. The law provides for registration to vote at any state or federal agency serving the public. This includes offices that issue driver's licenses (DMV), and public-assistance offices, such as Social Security. The law also provides for registration by mail without requiring a witness, and it prevents a voter from being dropped from the register for not voting. Some states are still in the process of implementing the law and you might find that requirements for state and local registration differ from Federal. However, most states have now complied. If you live in Minnesota, Wisconsin, Wyoming, New Hampshire or Idaho, you may register by mail or at the polls on the same day as an election. In North Dakota no registration is required in order to vote.

If you do not know the procedures for the state in which you live, call your local League of Women Voters, or your state's Department of Motor Vehicles.

THE FINAL FEW

Finally, notify religious organizations and business associations. And don't forget to send notifications to anyone who may send mail or publications to you. This includes newspapers, magazines, trade journals, professional journals, religious organizations, charitable organizations, business associates, and favorite catalogues. You will find contact information for the major publications listed below.

Note that some publications have customer service numbers and may take changes over the telephone. In addition to those listed below, you may find numbers listed in the publication or by calling toll-free information (1-800-555-1212) and asking for the customer service number for the specific publication. Even when done by phone, the change can sometimes take as long as 2 weeks.

If notifying the publication by mail, peel off the old address label from your magazine and include it with your new information.

KEY CONTACTS

Atlantic Monthly
Box 52661
Boulder, CO 80322

Business Week
P.O. Box 430
Hightstown, NJ 08520
1-800-635-1200

Cosmopolitan
1-800-888-2676

Entertainment Weekly
1-800-828-6882

Fortune
1-800-621-8000

Glamour
Box 53716
Boulder, CO 80322
1-800-274-7410

Gourmet
Box 53780
Boulder, CO 80322

Life
P.O. Box 30605
Tampa, FL 33630-0605
1-800-621-6000

Mademoiselle
Box 54348
Boulder, CO 80322
1-800-274-4750

Money
P.O. Box 30607
Tampa, FL 33630-0607
1-800-633-9970

Newsweek
The Newsweek Building
Livingston, NJ 07039-1666
1-800-631-1040

People
P.O. Box 30603
Tampa, FL 33630-0603
1-800-541-1000

Readers Digest
Pleasantville, NY 10570
1-800-234-9000

Redbook
Box 7190
Red Oak, IA 51591
1-800-888-0008

Self
1-800-274-6111

Time
P.O. Box 30601
Tampa, FL 33630-0601
1-800-843-8463

TV Guide
Box 900
Radnor, PA 19088
1-800-345-8500

U.S. News & World Report
1-800-334-1313

Wall Street Journal
1-800-568-7625
Fax: 1-413-592-4782

Working Woman
P.O. Box 3274
Harlan, IA 51593-0454
1-800-234-9675

Vanity Fair
Box 53516
Boulder, CO 80322
1-800-365-0635

Vogue
Box 55980
Boulder, CO 80322
1-800-234-2347

APPENDIX A

𝒦ey 𝒞ontacts
(𝒜lphabetical 𝓛isting)

The following section is an alphabetical listing of organizations you are most likely to need notification of name changes. These organizations are listed throughout the book in the appropriate category and are provided here as a handy reference. The contacts included here provide a sampling of the most popular and often requested organizations.

Alamo Rent A Car
Quick Silver Club
1-800-732-3232
Fax: 1-800-851-5246

Allstate Motor Club
1-800-255-2582 or
1-800-347-8880

American Express
1-800-528-4800

American Airlines AAdvantage
MD 5400
P.O. Box 619620
Dallas/Fort Worth Airport,
Texas 75261-9620
1-800-882-8880

American Automobile
Association (AAA)
Call the local number on your membership card or check the telephone directory. Be sure to use the correct local name such as "Automobile Club of Michigan" or "New Jersey Automobile Club". If unsure, call 1-800-222-4357 and you will be referred to the correct local club.

Amoco
1-800-247-0067

Amoco Motor Club
1-800-334-3300

AT&T Universal
1-800-423-4343

Atlantic Monthly
Box 52661
Boulder, CO 80322

Avis Rent A Car System
Wizard Club
Customer Service Center
900 Old Country Road
Garden City, NY 11530
1-800-352-7900

BankAmerica
Look for number on your
statement, if unsure, call
1-800-227-5458 or
1-800-243-7762

BP
1-800-222-1005

Beau's
941-747-2355

Bloomingdale's
212-705-2000

The Bon Marche
206-506-6000

The Bon-Ton
717-757-7660

Burdines
305-835-5151

Business Week
P.O. Box 430
Hightstown, NJ 08520
1-800-635-1200

Carson Pirie Scott
414-347-4141

Chase Manhattan
1-800-441-7681

Chevron
1-510-602-7020

Chevron Travel Club
1-800-255-2273

Citibank
1-800-950-5114

Continental OnePass Service
Center
P.O. Box 4365
Houston, TX 77210-4365
1-713-952-1630

Cosmopolitan
1-800-888-2676

Cross Country Motor Club
1-800-225-1575

Delta Airlines, Inc.
Frequent Flyer Service
Center
Hartsfield Atlanta Int'l
Airport - Dept. 745
P.O. Box 20532
Atlanta, GA 30320-2532
1-800-323-2323

Dillard's
501-376-5200

Diner's Club
1-800-525-9135

Discover Card
1-800-347-2683

Driver's License and Motor Vehicle
Registration
Look in the state government listings
in your telephone directory under
Motor Vehicle Division for your
nearest office

Elder-Beerman
513-296-2700

Entertainment Weekly
1-800-828-6882

Equifax Credit Bureau
1-800-685-1111

Exxon
1-800-344-4355

Exxon Travel Club
1-800-833-9966

Filene's
617-537-2978

Foley's
713-651-7038

Fortune
1-800-621-8000

Glamour
Box 53716
Boulder, CO 80322
1-800-274-7410

Gottschalks
209-434-8000

Gourmet
Box 53780
Boulder, CO 80322

Hecht's
703-558-1200

Herberger's
612-251-5351

The Hertz Corporation
#1 Club
P.O. Box 25991
Oklahoma City, OK 73126
1-800-227-4653

I. Magnin
1-800-726-3444

Immigration and
Naturalization
Look in the U.S.
Government pages of your
telephone directory under
Immigration and
Naturalization Service (INS)
or under the Department of
Justice heading

Internal Revenue Service
1-800-829-1040

J.C. Penney
1-800-542-0800

Jacobson's
517-764-6400

John Wanamaker
1-800-333-0170

Kohl's
414-783-5800

Lazarus
404-913-4000

Life
P.O. Box 30605
Tampa, FL 33630-0605
1-800-621-6000

The Limited
P.O. Box 182123
Columbus, OH 43283
1-800-888-3257

Lord & Taylor
424 5th Avenue
New York, NY 10018
Attn.: Customer Svc
1-212-827-5200

Macy's
1-800-743-6229

Mademoiselle
Box 54348
Boulder, CO 80322
1-800-274-4750

Marathon
1-800-537-9580

Marshall Field's
312-781-1000

McRae's
601-968-4400

Mervyn's
510-785-8800

Mobil
1-800-225-9547

Mobil Automobile Club
1-800-621-5581

Money
P.O. Box 30607
Tampa, FL 33630-0607
1-800-633-9970

Montgomery Ward
1-800-289-9740

Montgomery Ward Auto Club
1-800-621-5151

National Car Rental
Emerald Club
7700 Franc Avenue S.
Minneapolis, MN 55435
1-800-962-7070

Neiman Marcus
214-741-6911

Newsweek
The Newsweek Building
Livingston, NJ 07039-1666
1-800-631-1040

Nordstrom
206-628-2111

Northwest Airlines, Inc.
World Perks Service Center
P.O. Box 11001
St. Paul, MN 55111-0001
1-800-327-2881

Parisian
205-940-4000

Peebles
804-447-5200

People
P.O. Box 30603
Tampa, FL 33630-0603
1-800-541-1000

Readers Digest
Pleasantville, NY 10570
1-800-234-9000

Redbook
Box 7190
Red Oak, IA 51591
1-800-888-0008

Rich's
1-800-241-0488

Road America Motor Club
1-800-262-7262

Robinsons-May
818-508-5226

Saks Fifth Avenue
1-800-221-8340

Sears, Roebuck and Co.
Call the 800 number on your
monthly statement

Self
1-800-274-6111

Shell
1-800-331-3703

Shell Motorist Club
1-800-621-8663

Social Security
1-800-772-1213

Spiegel
1-800-345-4500

Stern's
201-845-5500

Sunoco
1-800-331-8850

Texaco
1-800-552-7827

Time
P.O. Box 30601
Tampa, FL 33630-0601
1-800-843-8463

TRW Credit Bureau
1-800-682-7654

TransUnion Credit Bureau
1-800-851-2674

TV Guide
Box 900
Radnor, PA 19088
1-800-345-8500

TWA - FFB
P.O. Box 800
Fairview Village, PA 19409
1-800-325-4815

United Airlines
Mileage Plus Service Center
P.O. Box 28870
Tucson, AZ 85726-8870

USAir
Frequent Traveler Program
Service Center
P.O. Box 65
Winston-Salem, NC
27102-0065
1-800-USAIRFT (872-4738)

U.S. News & World Report
1-800-334-1313

U.S. Passport
Look in your telephone directory
in the federal government
frequently called numbers list or
under U.S. Department of State
to find your nearest office

U.S. Savings Bonds
Contact your local bank or
Department of the Treasury
U.S. Savings Bonds Division
Washington, D.C. 20226.
1-202-377-7700

Wall Street Journal
1-800-568-7625
Fax: 1-413-592-4782

Working Woman
P.O.Box 3274
Harlan, IA 51593-0454
1-800-234-9675

Vanity Fair
Box 53516
Boulder, CO 80322
1-800-365-0635

Vogue
Box 55980
Boulder, CO 80322
1-800-234-2347

Younkers
515-244-1112

APPENDIX B

The Checklist and Change Record

This chart is provided to help you document changes quickly and provide a follow-up record to use until the changes are complete. When you have finished you not only will have a complete checklist of your changes but, if you keep and maintain it, you will have a document that will continue to be useful as a record of your memberships, accounts, policies, identification numbers, and affiliations.

TO USE THE CHECKLIST AND CHANGE RECORD

1. Enter the organization or company you are notifying under the appropriate category heading.

2. Enter any corresponding reference number, (e.g., account, policy or membership).

3. Make an ✓ to indicate whether you are notifying of a change of name, address, or both.

4. Enter the date of each contact made, and whether by phone, mail, in person, or by fax, under the appropriate column.

5. If you made contact by telephone, indicate the name of the person with whom you spoke and the telephone number.

6. List all documents provided and check if they are originals.

7. Make an ✓ to indicate when a document has been returned to you.

8. Note any useful information or additional requirements, telephone numbers, addresses, etc.

9. Make an ✓ when the entire notification process for an item is completed.

An example (with numbers corresponding to the numbered instructions above) has been provided on the chart to help you. In this instance, the bride (Alice) has telephoned her bank to confirm their requirements. Alice entered the bank name (1) and her account number (2), and indicated that she is changing both her name and address (3). On June 8 (4), Alice spoke with Mary Chase at the bank and noted her phone number (5). Ms. Chase told her she would need a certified copy of her marriage certificate, completed signature cards and a driver's license for identification (6). Ms. Chase instructed Alice to bring these items to the bank in person and told her that her marriage certificate would be returned to her after the changes were made. Alice noted this and also that she is adding her husband, Jeff, to the account (8). Alice went to the bank on June 15 (4), to make the changes and when she received the marriage certificate back from the bank (7), she marked this notification process complete (9).

❦ TAKE NOTE! ❦
Photocopy the following charts; they'll be much easier to use!

Checklist & Change Record

	Reference or Account Number	✓ Name Change	✓ Address Change	Date of Contact	✓ Phone	✓ Mail	✓ Fax	✓ In Person	Contact Name & Phone Number
Company or Organization									
***Example:* First Union Bank** ①	000-123-456 ②	✓③	✓③	6/8/95 ④ 6/15/95 ④	✓			✓	**Mary Chase** ⑤ **555-9876**
Key Notifications:									
Social Security									
Driver's License									
Passport									
Employer									
Other									
Financial Institutions:									
Banks & Credit Unions									
Mortgage Company									
Investment Company									
Stock Broker									

Document(s) Sent	✔ Original Sent	✔ Returned	Notes	✔ Complete
Marriage Certificates ⑥	✔	✔	**Added Jeff to account** ⑧	✔
Driver's Lic., Sig. Cards	⑥	⑥	**Marriage Certificate to be Returned**	⑨

Checklist & Change Record	Reference or Account Number		Name Change	Address Change	Date of Contact		Phone	Mail	Fax	In Person		Contact Name & Phone Number
Company or Organization												
Savings Bonds												
Credit Cards:												
Retail Credit Cards												
Bank Credit Cards												
Gasoline Credit Cards												
Insurance:												
Life												
Accident												
Automobile												
Health												

Document(s) Sent	✓ Original Sent	✓ Returned	Notes	✓ Complete

Checklist & Change Record

Company or Organization	Reference or Account Number	Name Change	Address Change	Date of Contact	Phone	Mail	Fax	In Person	Contact Name & Phone Number
Company or Organization									
Mortgage									
Homeowners/ Renters									
Other									
Professionals:									
Doctor									
HMO/PPO									
Dentist									
Attorney									
Accountant									
Other									
Memberships:									
Alumni Association									
Auto Club									
Book Club									
Car Rental Clubs									

Document(s) Sent	Original Sent	Returned	Notes	Complete

Checklist & Change Record	Reference or Account Number	Name Change	Address Change	Date of Contact	Phone	Mail	Fax	In Person	Contact Name & Phone Number
Company or Organization									
Car Rental Clubs Cont'd									
Frequent Flyer Clubs									
Health Club									
Investment Club									
Library									
Professional Association									
Video/Music Club									
Video Store									
Other									
Not To Be Forgotten:									
Voter Registration									
Check Cashing Card									

Document(s) Sent	✔ Original Sent	✔ Returned	Notes	✔ Complete

Checklist & Change Record	Reference or Account Number	Name Change	Address Change	Date of Contact	Phone	Mail	Fax	In Person	Contact Name & Phone Number
Company or Organization									
Religious Organization									
Business Associates									
Subscriptions & Catalogs									
Miscellaneous:									

Document(s) Sent	✓ Original Sent	✓ Returned	Notes	✓ Complete

Notice of Change

Please make the following change(s) to my account:

Account Number: _____

Account Name on Record: _____

New Name: _____
❑ Proof of marriage is attached.

Address: _____

City/State/Zip Code: _____
❑ This is a new address.

Thank you,
Signature: _____   **Date:** _____

Notice of Change

Please make the following change(s) to my account:

Account Number: _____

Account Name on Record: _____

New Name: _____
❑ Proof of marriage is attached.

Address: _____

City/State/Zip Code: _____
❑ This is a new address.

Thank you,
Signature: _____   **Date:** _____

$\mathcal{I}$NDEX

Do You Take This... Name?
The Bride's Complete Guide to
Choosing and Changing Her Name

can be ordered through your local bookseller,

or by sending check or money order with this form to:
American Literary Press, Inc.
8019 Belair Road, Suite 10
Baltimore, Maryland 21236

- -

Do You Take This... Name?
The Bride's Complete Guide to
Choosing and Changing Her Name

I would like to order _____ copies of *Do You Take This Name?* at $14.95 each. Enclosed is a check or money order for _____. (Be sure to include $3.00 for shipping and handling for the first copy, $1.00 each additional copy. Maryland residents add 5% sales tax.

Name _____

Address _____

City _____ State _____ Zipcode _____

American Literary Press, Inc.
Five Star Special Edition
8019 Belair Road, Suite 10 • Baltimore, Maryland 21236
Ordering Information: (410)882-7700 • 1(800)873-2003 out of area
9:00 a.m. to 5:00 p.m. (ET)
amerlit@erols.com